Wee Willie Winkie
Runs through the town,
Upstairs and downstairs
In his night-gown,
Rapping at the window,
Crying through the lock,
'Are the children all in bed,
For now it's eight o'clock?'

Barefoot Books
PO Box 95
Kingswood
Bristol
BS15 5BH

Graphic design by Jennifer Hoare
Colour separation by Scanner Services, Verona
Printed in Singapore by Tien Wah Press [Pte] Ltd

ISBN 1 901223 45 0

Hush, Little Baby

Lullabies for Bedtime

∾

Illustrated by Margaret Walty

BAREFOOT BOOKS
BATH

Contents

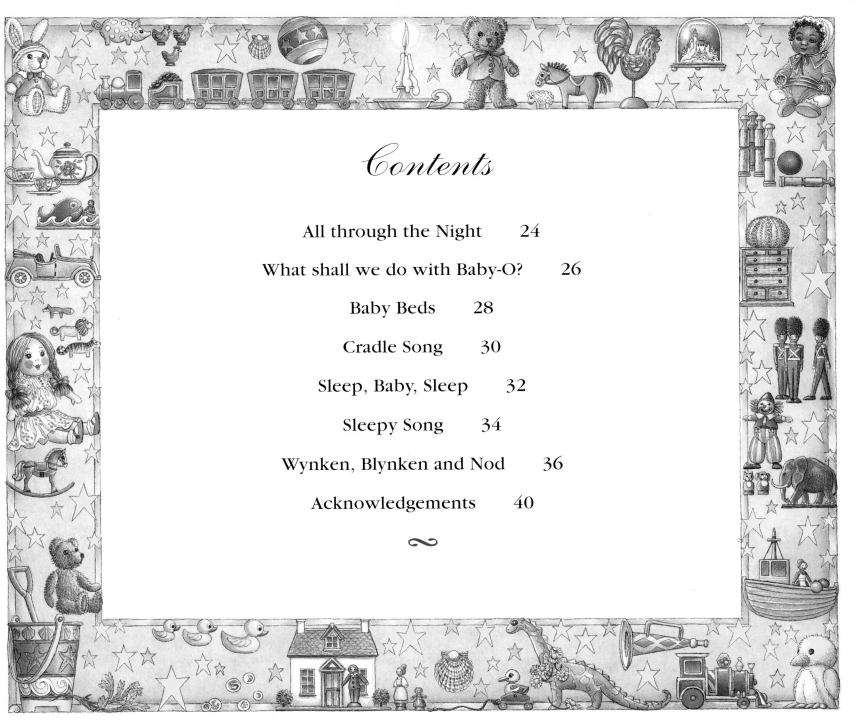

Contents

Brahms' Lullaby

Lulla - by and good - night, in the sky stars are bright. Round your head flow - ers gay, scent your slum - bers till day. Close your eyes now and rest, may these hours be blest. Go to sleep now and rest, may these hours be blest.

When the blazing sun is set,
When the grass with dew is wet,
Then you show your little light,
Twinkle, twinkle, all the night.
Twinkle, twinkle, little star,
How I wonder what you are.

Then the traveller in the dark,
Thanks you for the tiny spark,
He could not see which way to go,
If you did not twinkle so.
Though I know not what you are,
Twinkle, twinkle, little star.

Far in the Wood

Far in the wood you'll find a well, with wa-ter

deep and clear. Who-e - ver drinks by

moon - light bright, will live a thou - sand year,

will live a thou - sand year.

And all around the little well,
Are seven lovely trees.
They rock and sway and sing a song,
And whisper in the breeze,
And whisper in the breeze.

And through the seven little trees,
The evening wind will blow
And down fall seven little dreams,
My baby all for you,
My baby all for you.

All the Pretty Little Horses

Hush - you - bye, don't you cry, go to sleep - y, lit - tle

ba - by. When you wake, you shall have

all the pret - ty lit - tle hor - ses — blacks and bays,

dap - ples and grays, coach and six - a lit - tle hor - ses.

13

Evening Song

the wave rocks the li - ly, the wind

rocks the tree. And I rock the ba - by so

soft - ly to sleep, she must

not a - wa - ken till dai - sy buds peep.

A Spell for Sleeping

Se - ven fish in the sway of wa - ter. Six can-dles for a

king's daugh - ter. Five sighs for a droo - ping head.

Four ghosts to gen - tle her bed. Three owls in the

dusk fall - ing. Two tales to be tell - ing.

One spell for sleep - ing.

Sweet and Low

Sweet and low, sweet and low, wind of the west-ern

sea,——— low, low, breathe and blow,

wind of the west-ern sea, ——— o - ver the roll - ing

18

wa - ters go, come from the dy - ing moon, and blow,

blow him a - gain to me; —————— while my lit - tle one,

while my pret - ty one sleeps. —————————

19

Hush, Little Baby

Hush, li-ttle ba-by, don't say a word,

Pa-pa's going to buy you a mock-ing bird. And

if that mock-ing bird don't sing,

Pa-pa's going to buy you a dia-mond ring.

20

And if that diamond ring turns to brass,
Papa's going to buy you a looking-glass.

And if that looking-glass gets broke,
Papa's going to buy you a billy-goat.

And if that billy-goat don't pull,
Papa's going to buy you a cart and bull.

And if that cart and bull turn over,
Papa's going to buy you a dog named Rover.

And if that dog named Rover don't bark,
Papa's going to buy you a horse and cart.

And if that horse and cart fall down,
You'll still be the cutest little baby in town.

Rock~a~Bye Baby

Rock - a - bye ba - by   on   the tree top,

when the wind blows the   cra - dle will rock.

When the bough breaks the   cra - dle will fall,

down will come ba - by,   cra - dle and all.

22

All through the Night

Sleep my love, and peace att - end thee, all through the
night, guar - dian an - gels God will lend thee,
all through the night. Soft and drow - sy hours are cree - ping,
hill and dale in slum - ber slee - ping. Love a - lone his
watch is kee - ping, all through the night.

Sleep, my baby, sleep my darling,

All through the night.

On your cradle moon is shining,

All through the night.

God with me His watch is keeping,

Oh how gently you are sleeping,

Slumber softly while I rock you,

All through the night.

What shall we do with Baby~O?

What shall we do with ba - by - o, what shall we do with

ba - by - o, what shall we do with ba - by - o,

if he won't go to slee - py - o? Wrap him up in

ca - li - co, ca - li - co, wrap him up in ca - li - co,

26

send him to his mum - my - o. What shall we do with

ba - by - o, what shall we do with ba - by - o,

what shall we do with ba - by - o, if he won't go to

slee - py - o?

Baby Beds

Li - ttle lambs, li - ttle lambs, where do you sleep?

In the green mea-dow with mo - ther sheep. Li - ttle birds,

li - ttle birds, where do you rest? Close to our mo - ther in a

warm nest. Ba - by dear, ba - by dear, where do you lie?

In my warm bed with mo - ther close by.

Cradle Song

Sleep, my li-ttle one, sleep. Fa-ther is tend-ing the
sheep. Gar-den and mea-dow are still, cows are a-sleep on the
hill. See how the moon rides so high, sail-ing a-cross the
sky. Time to close your eyes. Sleep my li-ttle one, sleep.

31

Sleep, Baby, Sleep

Sleep, ba - by, sleep, sleep, ba - by sleep, your

fa - ther tends the sheep. Your mo - ther shakes the

dream - land tree, soft - ly fall sweet dreams for thee,

sleep, ba - by, sleep, sleep, ba - by, sleep.

Sleep, baby, sleep,
Sleep, baby, sleep,
The large stars are the sheep.
The little stars are the lambs, I guess,
And the gentle moon is the shepherdess,
Sleep, baby, sleep, sleep, baby, sleep.

Sleep, baby, sleep,
Sleep, baby, sleep,
Down where the wood bines creep.
Be always like the lamb so mild,
A kind, and sweet, and gentle child,
Sleep, baby, sleep, sleep, baby, sleep.

33

Sleepy Song

Hush - a - bye ba - by Da - ddy's a - way,

bro - thers and sis - ters have gone out to play, but

here by your cra - dle, dear ba - by I'll keep, to

guard you from dan - ger and sing you to sleep.

Wynken, Blynken and Nod

Wynken, Blynken and Nod one night

Sailed off in a wooden shoe –

Sailed on a river of crystal light,

Into a sea of dew.

'Where are you going, and what do you wish?'

The old moon asked the three.

'We have come to fish the herring fish

That live in this beautiful sea:

Nets of silver and gold have we!'

Said Wynken,

Blynken,

And Nod.

36

The old moon laughed and sang a song,
As they rocked in the wooden shoe,
And the wind that sped them all night long
Ruffled the waves of dew.
The little stars were the herring fish
That lived in that beautiful sea –
'Now cast your nets wherever you wish –
Never afeared are we;'
So cried the stars to the fishermen three:
Wynken,
Blynken,
and Nod.

37

All night long their nets they threw
To the stars in the twinkling foam –
Then down from the skies came the wooden shoe,
Bringing the fishermen home;
'Twas all so pretty a sail it seemed
As if it could not be,
And some folks thought 'twas a dream they'd dreamed
Of sailing that beautiful sea –
But I shall name you the fishermen three:
Wynken,
Blynken,
And Nod.

Wynken and Blynken are two little eyes,
And Nod is a little head,
And the wooden shoe that sailed to the skies
Is a wee one's trundle bed.
So shut your eyes while your mother sings
Of wonderful sights that be,
And you shall see the beautiful things
As you rock in the misty sea,
Where the old shoe rocked and the fishermen three:
Wynken,
Blynken,
And Nod.

39

Acknowledgements

The publishers wish to thank Lavinia Ferguson for sourcing and
checking the piano music to accompany these lullabies.

Grateful acknowledgement is also made to the following composers
and publishers for their permission to reproduce material
copyrighted or controlled by them:

The Children's Group Inc., for 'Cradle Song', copyright © by Classical Kids [1992]
adapted from *Daydreams and Lullabies* CD.

Michael Joseph for 'Sweet and Low', taken from *The Parlour Song Book* [1972]
and composed by Sir Joseph Barnby.

The publishers have made every effort to contact holders of copyright
material. If you have not received our correspondence,
please contact us for inclusion in future editions.